Colors
at
Work

*Enrich your life at work
through the tools and
insights of Colors*

George J. Boelcke, CCP

Also by George Boelcke:

- Colorful Personalities: Discover Your
  Personality Type Through the Power of Colors
- Colorful Personalities: Audio CD
- The Colors of Leadership and Management
- The Colors of Sales and Customers
- The Colors of Relationships
- The Colors of Parent and Child Dynamics
- Colors Tools for Christians
- It's Your Money! Tools, Tips and Tricks
  to Borrow Smarter and Pay It Off Quicker
  (www.yourmoneybook.com)

To Contact the Author:

George Boelcke facilitates seminars throughout North America and into Europe for organizations ranging from Fortune 500 firms to small businesses, church groups, relationship seminars, conventions, and schools. He can be contacted via:

E-mail: george@vantageseminars.com
Web-site:www.vantageseminars.com

Library and Archives Canada Cataloguing in Publication

Boelcke, George J., 1959–
      Colors at work : enrich your life at work through the tools and
      insights of colors / George J. Boelcke.

Includes index.

ISBN: 978-0-9784570-4-4

      1. Job enrichment--Psychological aspects. 2. Quality of work
      life--Psychological aspects. 3. Personality. 4. Work environment--
      Psychological aspects. 5. Color--Psychological aspects. I. Title.

      HF5549.5.J616B63 2012   158.2'6   C2012-903921-7

Layout & typeset by: Ingenieuse Productions, Edmonton, AB
Cover "wall" picture used with permission of Ratko Jagodic, Electronic
Visualization Laboratory, University of Illinois at Chicago
Edited by: Christina Heinze
Printed and bound in the United States of America

Contents

*"Our people matter" is something every company promotes.
But not all walk the walk.*

*I am blessed to work with many clients who consistently
and continuously practice putting their people first.
Especially:*

Mike, Steve, Cindy, Jenn, Aida & Shelley

Dan, Laura, Treena & Beata

Peter, Scott, Susan, Angela, Kerry, Kim & Kris

Marcie, Maxine, Greg, Taryn, Rhea & Michelle

*Maybe it's a coincidence that a large number of them are in
the "Best Companies to Work For," "Best Managed Companies,"
or "Best for Training and Development"...
or about to get there...*

*...or maybe Colors plays an integral part in making
"our people matter."*

First Things First

The trouble with other people is that they don't fit our templates, and don't see or live life the way we do. Their values and priorities are different from ours, they don't act, think, or behave like us, and they don't even make decisions the *right* way, or the way we think they should be made.

We are different: not better, not worse, just different. We value different things and have very different definitions of success or happiness. We are really good at many things, but get stressed out over different issues or behaviors. What we want or need or tend to focus on is not the same as most other people – at home or at work.

We have different motivators and certainly have four very distinct definitions of success, fun, being organized, and even working with other people.

Our personality types protect us and create safety for us. They create our comfort zone and make us different from others. Our personality may cause us to resist change or to label others. It is our compass and guide to life and shapes our values, priorities, and views on how life should be lived.

As a result, life within the four unique Colors can cause us confusion or misunderstandings. When we don't understand, that we inherently are four very different Colors, we may jump easily into judgments, or label another person as wrong. Either choice could quickly lead to trouble and communication breakdown, causing dysfunctional teams to form in any department, branch, or company.

It may take some time for some of us to realize our own real Colors. We can all wear masks to hide our scars, our true selves, and things we don't want others to see. Some of us mask our true Colors in the

false belief that people would find us unlovable
if they saw the real person inside.

Unfortunately, no graph, chart, or template will help us understand our different personality types. Sorry. There isn't even a formula to getting others to come around to our ways of thinking or acting, or a 5 or 7 step plan to make people be more, or less, like us.

We are as unique as our fingerprints and we cannot take all seven billion people in the world and break them down into four neat little groups. With each of our primary Color's behaviors, strengths, stresses, priorities, and communication styles, it's as though we speak four totally different languages. However, the *language* of our Color is not just the way we talk, it's also the way we work, coach, manage, and interact with others. It's the key to making us feel engaged and part of a team.

So, if we *speak* Spanish, it becomes critical that we understand the people whose first Color is not the same as ours and who don't *speak* Spanish at all! If we choose not to understand the *language* of their Colors, what do we think the odds are of ever successfully working with them in a cohesive team where everyone needs to pull together in the same direction?

Most of us tend to live mainly within our first two Colors. Depending on how close the scores of the Colors are, it might even be three. (The full Colors assessment and all the basics of Colors are in the Colorful Personalities book.) However, it is quite common that two Color's scores will be pretty high and two will tend to be on the lower end. Our first Color reflects the behaviors, values, and strengths that come naturally to us. Our first Color is how we would like the world to function, what we would like the Color of our manager to be, and what would ideally be the Color we would work in for most of the day.

Our second Color is often how we express or live our first Color. It can also be the place where we *hide* under stress or in difficult times. On the other extreme, our last Color is the hardest to relate to, and will cause us the greatest challenges – but also the greatest opportunities for growth. Let's face it – while it might be our lowest Color, there are millions of people who have it as their highest score – which is why personality conflicts and judgements begin...

Will we make the effort and take the time to understand and value others? We have time every day to make it to work. Every day we take the time to get ready in the morning to look good, shower, and get dressed. We take care of ourselves by taking the time to have at least two or three meals a day, taking time to go out with our friends, and taking time to watch our favorite TV shows.

Many of us will not hesitate to take a year to learn a new sport, take four years to earn a degree or an apprenticeship, allow five years to earn a promotion, or set aside almost two decades to raise children. Yet somehow we believe our relationships at work should grow stronger and deeper without investing that same time and energy?

Invest the time! Use the tools of Colors and share the energy that we apply to our relationships to also invest in our work-relationships with our coworkers and bosses. It's worth it, and it will be one of the best investments we may ever make.

With the tools and insights of Colors, we must give ourselves permission to stop trying to change people. We must put in more than we take away, or want back in return.

We must focus less on what's *not* there, and rather build and expand on what *is* there – what other people contribute in terms of talents and skills. We'll be far more successful working on a team and in a department with the awesome talents of our Colors working together, than expending the time and energy in futile attempts to make other people more like ourselves.

Let's make it less about right and wrong and more about doing what works; less about the process or how-to, and more about the final result and where to get to!

No matter what our scores, every one of us is a combination of all four Colors. And because our third and fourth colors are less utilized, we frequently deny or downplay the talents we have within ourselves from these lower Colors. Imagine if we didn't downplay these talents. We'd be forced to utilize all those hidden talents, and acknowledge the diverse talents we didn't think we had.

In terms of our two highest Colors, we also seldom acknowledge or celebrate our natural gifts and strengths. After all, they come so easily to us. It's not a big deal that we totally underestimate or undervalue them. It is often in our interaction with other Colors that someone points out how great we are at certain things; things which are much more challenging for others to accomplish. We believe that those great things that we do all the time, and have for a lifetime – can't be anything special. Let's give ourselves credit for the natural talents and gifts of our Colors. After all, part of the definition of self-esteem is feeling great about us. After we take care of our physical needs, our self-esteem is one of the most important factors in our lives.

Even our lives at work necessitate all four Colors at various times and in various situations. Anyone of us can be successful in any career. Colors have nothing to do with talents or IQs, and the positions we have at work do not define our Colors, nor do they turn us into a different Color. Whether it's at work, as a parent, or in many other areas of our lives – sometimes we just need to do what needs to be done. That doesn't change our personality types – it just means we need to take on the roll of a different Color. When we choose to utilize the strengths of all of our Colors, we become well-rounded and create life in balance where:

Our Blue consistently shows in our caring and helping of others. We involve everyone around us and give from the heart – to our teams and others. Our kindness and communication skills touch those we come into contact with; and we make everyone feel welcome and included.

Our genuine warmth, empathy, and teamwork skills are contagious and impact everyone on our teams. We build lasting friendships and are always ready and willing to take time to help others.

Our Gold stands out in our loyalty and dependability in taking on tasks and seeing them through to completion. Our sense of right and wrong, our work ethic, and our planning skills are qualities that are important in our careers.

We don't just do it – we do it right, and we work systematically towards our goals. Our word is always good and we function well to meet deadlines without requiring a lot of supervision. We work as individuals and as team players, and can always be counted on to pitch in.

Our Orange is the energy of our teams and well beyond. We have a contagious sense of humor and teach others through our practical actions, high energy levels, and positive outlooks – always believing that anything is possible. We never shy away from a challenge, goal, or contest.

Our ability to multi-task, and our talents of flexibility without stress, are valued and envied by those that watch us in action. We are never afraid to roll up our sleeves and get involved in practical and creative ways that only we can pull off.

Our Green pursues challenges and solutions. We constantly seek improvements and keep our eyes on the big picture and broader vision. Our range of knowledge goes far beyond our job description and is well respected by those we work with.

We enjoy research, learning, and the chance to teach others by giving them the tools and knowledge to succeed. We continuously look for opportunities to share our broad knowledge and well thought-out ideas and suggestions with others.

The Power of Teamwork

Understanding Colors at work is one-half awareness and one-half what you choose to do with that knowledge.

Teamwork makes the dream work. At least that's the case for Blues. For the rest of the world, teamwork isn't about the *ability* to work together – it's about the willingness. And working *together* is entirely different than working as a team.

Every day at work we are part of a team in some way or another. The question is not whether we will participate in something that involves others; the question is whether our involvement with others will be successful. The success of our teams, and the productivity and atmosphere of the entire company, depends on the answer to that question. That question matters a lot to everyone's success.

The beautiful Clydesdale horses most people remember from the Budweiser commercials are able to pull about 8,000 pounds each. However, two of these horses working together, and having been taught to coordinate with each other, can actually pull 25,000 pounds! When we understand, believe, and practice the power of working together it makes an old African Proverb come true: *If you want to go fast, go alone. If you want to go far, go together.*

Each team, every department, and all companies, are like an imaginary jigsaw puzzle with all the four pieces (Colors) working together. Without one or the other, being successful is next to impossible over the long term. Different Colors have very different strengths and talents which are all critical to our success. They aren't better, they don't reflect or measure experience or IQ, but they are all an integral part of our success. If we choose to make our contribution by getting our entire team on the same wavelength and pulling in the same direction, we would be unstoppable in any career or business venture.

How would we feel about being employed at one of the 'Best Companies'? These 'Best Companies' ratings are annual rankings by major magazines and others. If we're like most people, who wouldn't want to be employed by one? However, these companies aren't mainly chosen by the perks they offer.

Furthermore, their employee's pay is almost always in the same range as other companies. But a large part of what does make these companies so desirable is their cultures – employees enjoying their jobs, having fun, feeling engaged, the acceptance and inclusion of others, and the growth of trusting relationships. That foundation starts with teamwork and building *effective* teams. That's not purely an H.R. mandate!

That starts with us, choosing to want to have that type of environment. If it is meant to be – it's up to me.

Relationships matter in all our dealings with coworkers, including those with our managers. Think of a boss or company that we really enjoyed working for. What was the most important reason we liked it? Think of a favorite restaurant. What brings us back? It's almost always the places with great service and with staff that really seem to care – who seem to enjoy their jobs and make us feel welcome, included, and special. Feeling valued is one of the most important common denominators in all of our experiences and a key reason for our loyalty.

Acceptance is definitely the more challenging part of the equation. People tend to get their backs up over differences in others. We are quite sure that others would fit in better if they just worked more like us. Utilizing Colors, time and again, is one of the best tools and methods to understanding these differences and achieving teamwork. Our personality differences may create stress, conflict, and confrontation. However, teamwork and unity come about when there is genuine appreciation for diversity.

Understanding these differences makes any group work well together. Some team members excel in building relationships with customers, while others deal well with crisis and managing problems. Another group is very detail-oriented and another can better see the big picture. Many contribute in building effective teams through their great sense of humor, high energy, creativity, determination, and unwavering positive attitudes.

What's our Color's primary goal at work? Is it that everything should be done together as a team? Done quickly and efficiently? As-planned and on the to-do list? Or done right the first time? If we answered yes to more than one of these, that's great news! Our lives at work happen in more than one Color!

Imagine how one-dimensional our teams would be if everyone was only one Color? What would we miss out on? What would fall by the wayside? We often don't see these multi-dimensional benefits when we focus on what sets us apart rather than on what binds us together. The great news is that there are a lot of things each of the Colors share with one another which bring cohesiveness even among two very different Colors:

Blue & Orange: are both very people-oriented, good negotiators, and effective problem solvers. They share a sense of optimism by focusing on the brighter side of things. Both value being liked, fitting in, and being recognized – Blues through verbal and meaningful personal ways, Oranges through concrete rewards like money or prizes.

Orange & Green: enjoy competition – Greens against themselves or systems, Oranges with anyone they may have a chance to win against. Both are independent and need their own space to perform well. They like new ways of doing things – Greens for ingenuity and mental challenges, and Oranges for excitement and to avoid boredom.

Gold & Blue: are both very socially-responsible and give back to others by donating their time, talents, or money. Golds contribute through service clubs and volunteering, while Blues gravitate to causes that involve personal care of people or animals. Both relate well to others and are great caretakers. They are helpful, cooperative, and excellent team players.

Green & Blue: both focus first on the big picture, then on the details. They are more interested in processes than results, and both are highly creative – Blues in artistic ways, and Greens through their innovative talents. Blues help people; Greens help people become more efficient and grow their knowledge.

Gold & Orange: both share a strong sense of wanting things done. Golds want tasks completed so they can move on with their to-do list; Oranges want to move five or six things forward at the same time as they love to multi-task. They are both task-oriented, exist in the here and now, and deal with concrete issues. Both enjoy productive teamwork where things actually get done, not just talked about.

So you see... we aren't all that different from one another. Even two very different Colors share some common attributes which in turn builds cohesiveness into our teams.

The foundation of building effective teams involves us taking accountability for our parts of it. It involves us being able to resolve conflicts (see page 35), build relationships, and accept other Colors as integral parts of our teams.

Effective teams also require Colors trusting each other. While trust is foundational to any team, it can also be quite fragile and viewed differently among the Colors. Blues and Oranges are, by nature, very positive. Both Colors usually start on the assumption that everyone is generally trustworthy until they prove differently. Golds and Greens believe trust is something that needs to be earned. Trust may take some time to develop, and a title will not automatically make someone trustworthy.

For every Color, and for every person, actions always speak louder than words. In some cases, we have to be in the trenches with someone and successfully come out the other side together, before trust can develop. And if we're not there for someone's struggles, we can't expect to be there for their successes.

Our different combinations of Colors look for a variety of verbal and non-verbal clues, behaviors, and actions in building trust with others:

Is it safe to be open and honest?

Do our actions match our words? Do we have integrity and credibility?

Can we ask for help and receive it without judgment, impatience, or pushback?

Do we show our playful and fun side, or do we fear others won't respect us, or find us credible?

Are we making eye contact and really listening?

Do we trust we'll get the job done without micro-managing others?

Do we honor our word and keep our commitments?

Will we coach others, ask others, care about others, and include others?

Can we admit when we've made a mistake?

We Showed Our Colors!

I have to share this story as it is so obvious to see the Colors of our team in action. Each of our branches was asked to do a team poster. We wanted ours to be a 'family' theme with finger paint. No, none of the Gold or Green staff were in on that creative decision.

Then I thought: Even better – lets all put our hand prints on the poster, in the color of our highest Color! I wish you could have seen the faces of the staff when I told them!

Green: I haven't put my hand in paint since I was two, and I'm not going to start again now. (Oh, but yes you are…) Their look said it all.

Gold: I'll put my hand in the paint, then wipe off all the excess right away. And could you tell me which space is mine, and specifically where you want me to put it? Oh, I don't think I can fit my hand there without touching another – that won't be very neat. Of course, then ten minutes of cleaning up…

Blue: This is so touching... hands all over the place, all different, but all together. How beautiful and fun – makes me feel like a kid again. Oh look, my hand is touching that Gold hand. How beautiful and symbolic... This is awesome!

Orange: You want me to what? OK, hurry up. I'll slap my hand through this paint...whoops, who is cleaning up all that paint on the table? Oh well, someone will...and the drips from the table to the poster...never mind... Then: SLAP – right in the middle of the poster with the hand spread wide and droplets of paint splattering all over everyone else's print...oh, whatever.

So the poster is done. We Blues think it's beautiful and symbolic. The Greens won't look at it. The Golds are really upset that the Oranges splattered on it and made a mess. If it didn't make their hands dirty, they'd really prefer to do it again – a lot neater, and with them in charge! And the Oranges? Well, they haven't given it a thought since it was done. It was fun – but so yesterday.

— D.N. – SCU

Who knows what you'll see when you see someone else's point of view?

How Each Color
Shows Us They Care

Often we hear people say that another person 'must have a lot of Blue in them'. While we know what that means, we all *do* have a lot of Blue within each of us, no matter what our primary Color is! We are all Blue – and Green and Orange and Gold – in one order or another, at some point in our day.

Just like the words freedom, fun, family, or honesty have different definitions for each Color, our Blue comes out in various ways, and at different times, whether it's our first Color or our last! But when we have an understanding of Colors, we need to look for the very different ways our Blue side – the being nice, patient, caring, and compassionate part of us - can manifest itself:

For high Golds, their 'Blue' generally shows in doing concrete and specific tasks for others, since they value being helpful and cooperative. Golds avoid the limelight, and a large part of what they do for others, are things other Colors may not even notice. They take care of things, because it is the right thing to do, and because it needs doing. It's not about drawing attention to *them*; it's just about helping out. Golds, will show they care, generally more in the form of actions than by words alone.

High Greens show us their caring side by giving us advice and showing us better ways of doing things. Perhaps they share books, magazines, or web stories that will really help us grow in our careers, or help us learn something new. They care enough to want us to do better!

Most high Oranges will show they care through verbal feedback, positive affirmations, and by including others. They will use their great sense of humor and hands-on skills to pull us out of our current state, get us back on track, and help us look at the positive side of a situation. Since they know everybody, and everybody knows them, Oranges will also be a great help in getting us contacts and referrals, or simply talking up our successes with others and being our biggest cheerleaders.

The strengths and joys of each of the Colors contribute in their own unique and different 'Blue' ways towards helping us and showing they care. But it will always be up to us to find the ways of *their* language. Pay attention to the non-verbal clues and look for the value – look for the Blue – in all Colors. It's always present in a wide variety of subtle ways, and we'll find it if we just choose to look, listen, and see.

Blues show us they care, support, and value us through:
- Sharing their time and making us a priority – often (usually) over their own work or tasks
- Remembering the small personal things such as a birthday, a special anniversary, or a sick relative
- Spending quality time with us and including us in their plans, whether its coffee, lunch, or anything else
- Having empathy and sharing from their hearts to connect with us in meaningful and personal ways
- Asking open-ended questions and getting to know the real *us* behind our outer shells
- Actively listening by using eye contact when speaking with us, making us feel special and heard
- Providing emotional connections by following up and following through on conversations they have had with us
- Having open body language and offering the physical touch of a hug or soft hand on the shoulder or arm
- Providing unconditional support and talking us up, to make us look good in the eyes of others
- Focusing on the positive, always looking for the good in everything, and being our natural cheerleaders and genuine friends
- Crying with us as much as laughing with us

Golds show us they care, support, and value us through:
- Performing acts of service – doing tasks, stepping in, or helping us accomplish something

- Physically being there for us – making the time to be with us to listen and to assist
- Offering corrective feedback which may include comments perceived as negative: "That won't work, because…"
- Helping us remember the details by often using *don't forget*-type comments
- Assisting in the planning or development of concrete steps towards an idea, project, or plan
- Adding structure and order to something (resources, priorities, tools, etc.)
- Expressing their concern for our safety by doing something right
- Providing *what if* help by offering a plan B or backup idea if something goes off the rails
- Stepping in and taking on portions of the work, job, project, or problem
- Giving accolades and being our cheerleader and supporter

Oranges show us they care, support, and value us through:
- Displaying enthusiasm and cheerleading us when we try to accomplish something
- Creating a contagious passion
- Offering a positive attitude and not letting us focus on the negatives, what-if's, or possible pitfalls in a situation
- Involving and engaging us in whatever they do
- Using their networking skills to help us
- Changing their priorities for us – making the quality time to be with us
- Getting us to *just do it*, or *just go for it*, by not over-planning or worrying too much
- Adding their great creativity in anything
- Staying flexible and adding innovative ideas… as our plans, ideas, or projects may change
- Keeping us focused on the now – the immediacy of the project, and today's issues

Greens show us they care, support, and value us through:

- Giving us more information, new opportunities, and more responsibilities
- Adding the 'depth' to something, through coaching and research, backing it with articles, links, or other information
- Making us think... always...
- Challenging us to do better or more and never settling for less
- Adding credibility or growing the credibility of an idea, project, or plan
- Focusing on the facts and providing logic over feelings
- Holding us accountable
- Pointing out or making us think through potential pitfalls, problems, or hurdles
- Teaching us to think before talking and plan before walking
- Not deviating from their own high standards and expectations
- Caring enough to not let us default to a *good enough* attitude or approach
- Asking probing questions: why...? what if...? have you thought about...? why didn't you...?

Getting feedback from each Color

Why don't most, or at least more, employees offer up their feedback, suggestions, or ideas? According to a new study from Kansas University, there are good reasons. Often, it is because companies minimize, ignore, or forget the social ramifications involved with accepting great ideas.

The study found that social concerns often have employees choosing never to speak up. Feirong Yuan, one of the authors of the study, added that this trend is more common in companies or departments where, by perception or reality, the firm does not value change. In those organizations, even an employee who has a great idea may be reluctant to speak up, fearing that he or she will be seen as disruptive.

However, there are things companies, managers, or even individuals can do to become more like I.T. firms or start-ups, where everyone's new ideas are actively sought out, and almost made mandatory. Some firms create this open atmosphere through innovation, others through incorporating it into their employee evaluations. But the study found that one of the core ways to have individuals volunteer ideas, suggestions, and feedback is to first establish people of importance to positions where they will actively listen and welcome this feedback.

Blues can supply powerful insights into teamwork or customer service areas, as they intuitively know way more of what's going on among people than any other Color is able to.

Golds may not be the first Color to embrace change, but they are the best source for tweaking efficiencies, finding redundant work that can be eliminated, or offering huge cost-cutting measures. They visualize these improvements, they tell their friends, but more often than not, they won't share them publicly at work.

Oranges know many shortcuts to getting things done. *They're* using these shortcuts, so why would others not want to implement them? Oranges are also incredibly creative – if someone would just challenge them and give them motivation for doing so.

Greens are constantly thinking of new and better ways things could be done, implemented, or streamlined. While they are the least likely to be discouraged from providing their feedback, they stop being interested when they reason that nobody is listening or implementing any of their ideas.

Without knowing Colors, most people wouldn't know how to ask, who to ask, or how to make it a safe environment for each Color to contribute their unique strengths through powerful feedback and suggestions.

Dealing With The Boss

For better or worse, everyone of us has a boss, no matter what our title or job description. Even a CEO is ultimately accountable to a board of directors. Managers and leaders come in all different shapes, talents, genders, and yes, in all four colors too.

The more quickly our bosses and ourselves all understand and appreciate that everything at work is about 'let's make a deal', the fewer conflicts, stress, and misunderstandings we'll have. Even if we have a manager whose primary Color is identical to ours, we'd still have conflict. It would just be in different areas and about different issues than we may currently be experiencing.

One day, if not already, we'll be a supervisor or manager and will quickly realize that the goal of leading an entire team of mini-me's may make it easier to manage everyone, but it would be a totally dysfunctional and one-dimensional team. It would be missing three quarters of the natural skills and strengths that other Colors could be contributing to our success at work.

Supervisors, managers, and leaders have secrets they actually wish others would know...

They have many great ideas and big dreams for their teams. They get scared at times, and have real life *stuff* going on at home. They juggle a ton of needs and wants from customers, vendors, their teams, and their managers or directors. On top of all this, they have budgets, strategic plans, profitability plans, and effective-team plans to adhere to. They try to stay ahead of their growing e-mail inbox and deal with a host of other daily fires and hurdles.

It may only be a part-time job for our managers – 12 hours a day, instead of 24! It's never an easy job, and they're doing the best they can with what they have. Not to mention, they are also working with a wide variety of people with different experiences, talents, and Colors!

Blue managers care a lot about the social needs and teamwork within their departments. They are always cognizant of assuring that everyone is happy, valued, and included in all relevant team activities. They are the first to organize team and social functions, strengthening the bonds of their groups.

They are the great diplomats and know just what to say, when to say it, and most importantly, how to say it. Blue managers are patient in coaching their teams, use an open mind approach, and provide excellent motivational styles.

Not wanting to make waves, or become too domineering, they can also turn introverted and become rather quiet. Of course, there is no off switch to their feelings, which can sometimes have Blue managers wondering if they have done enough of something, or whether they could have done it differently. They often feel partly at fault when others have not performed up to par – taking ownership of the problems and pitfalls of others.

Gold managers are incredibly loyal and protective of their companies, as well as of their teams. They have a view of the world as being either black or white, which may not be shared by other Colors. However, their teams will always know where they stand and what the rules or expectations are.

While Gold managers certainly have high expectations, they are also very fair in their treatment of others, allocating the workload, and sharing the credit for successes. Gold managers may not seem like a lot of fun, in the typical sense of the word, but fun comes differently to all four Colors. For Golds, getting the work done smoothly, without hiccups or surprises, on time and on budget, *is* a lot of fun.

They value structure and a tried and tested approach. If they seem like they're not very receptive to new ideas, Golds may just need the time to think through the value and implications of any changes.

Oranges are the energy bosses. They value the big picture overview, and bottom-line results. No excuses or whining, just do it – whatever it takes! It's nothing more than they expect of themselves. Stuff needs to get done and results matter a lot, but *please* let's have some fun along the way.

They are constantly positive and always on the move with the natural ability to multi-task, maintain creativity, and supply unlimited amounts of energy. Their doors are always open and they're more than willing to kid around with their teams. They *always* have time for their employees.

Other Colors may not think something is reasonable, or capable of getting done, but Oranges stick to the task and get on with it. They are rather allergic to whiners and negative people and will quickly show it in words and other ways. Their niceties, handholding, and managing of some staff will have to wait – right now they have too much to do to notice.

Green managers are more interested in results and the final payoff by analyzing the specific details and *how* the results are achieved. They certainly excel at taking complex concepts, problems, or situations and bringing them down to real size by grasping what needs to be done and finding innovative solutions.

Behind the scenes, Green managers constantly look for ways to improve their efficiencies, increase their training budgets, and make their teams better, smarter, more efficient, and more knowledgeable.

Their calm and cool demeanor is certainly an asset under pressure, but also acts as a double-edged sword. Green managers are hard to get to know on a personal level, and are not interested in feeling-type conversations, or even an excessive amount of small talk.

Communicating and Succeeding With Our Boss

... and everybody else who shares that Color

With Blues:

Do:

Tell them how it will help

Show genuine interest

Engage them in conversation (active listening) & eye contact

First, show them that we care

Show empathy & sympathy

Speak openly

Be positive

Dream with them about the big picture

Make it about us & striving to create win-win outcomes

Be sensitive to their feelings & intuitive decisions

Ask open-ended questions

Look for shared values & interests

Don't:

Put the job, rules, policies, or tasks ahead of people

Become judgmental

Tear someone else down to build ourselves up

Avoid eye contact

Interrupt or cut them off

Answer our cell phone or text

Become critical

Be mean through gossip, words, or judgments

Look for one word answers

Raise our voices

Put the emphasis on the details

Jump into fixing over listening

Be pushy, rude, cold, or curt

With Golds:

Do:	Don't:
Stay business like	Waste their time
Get to the point & stay on topic	Break, bend, or ignore the rules
Keep them updated & informed	Procrastinate
Be on time & respect their time	Lose focus of reality & practicality
Stay concise & focused	Tell them what to do or how to do it
Be orderly & organized	Forget
Keep the small talk to a minimum	Get too personal
Follow the rules & procedures	Put them in the spotlight or single them out
Take responsibility for our actions	Misjudge their direct, business-like approach
It properly the first time – every time	Argue the facts
Be precise & direct	Pass the buck
Give them information in writing	Make excuses
Ask – don't tell or force	Think it's not black or white

With Orange:

Do:

Start with the big picture

Focus on 'What's in it for us'

Bring a sense of humor

Make it visual

Involve some recognition or a chance to shine

Stay positive with focus on how to *getter-done*

Remind them (and take care of) the details

Ask about their weekends or sports happenings

Make it into a 'win' for them

Be brief, be bright, and be gone

Focus on the 'today' issues & solutions

Summarize the highlights & the action plan

Give them time to talk & get involved hands-on

Don't:

Overload them with too many unnecessary details

Take too long

Make it a drama

Negatively motivate them (If you don't do this...)

Waste their time

Use excuses

Be so serious

Get hung up solely on the rules & procedures

Pull out the manuals

Bring our to-do lists out

Assume they're not highly intelligent

Feed back all the details from conversations

Take it personally that they may repeat or forget

With Greens:

Do:

Know the facts & stay focused on them

Get it right the first time

Listen properly

Make sense & be logical

Give them information

Allow for the time & space to make a decision

Do our due diligence & homework in advance

Be upfront, honest & direct

Give them all the details

Stay true to our word

Ask if we don't know or understand

Show them we want to learn, grow & succeed

Be accountable for your actions & results

Don't:

Rush, push, press, or 'sell' them

Be too casual

Kid around too much

Take offense from their sarcasm or direct questions

Hype or dream

Fake it or bluff it & 'I don't know' is never an answer

Get feelings involved

Force an issue or decision

Give ultimatums or either/or's

Cajole

Tell them a story

Misconstrue blunt answers with criticism

Assume silence equals agreement

When Your Strengths Turn to Trouble

Everyone has heard the expression 'too much of a good thing.' That certainly applies to the strengths and traits of our primary Colors when many things, taken a bit too far, can quickly turn to trouble.

Since we cannot change, or at least not dial back what we don't know, it becomes very powerful to be aware of some of our personality-strengths taken one step too far. The common strengths of our Colors are a huge blessing, but what happens when we impose them on others? How quickly will we get pushback, or quite rightly, have others get their backs up?

The following are some common trouble issues which arise out of the strengths of our primary Colors. Most importantly is for us to be aware of at least two specific issues which apply to us *personally*:

What can make trouble for **Blues**?

- Shutting down, giving in, and usually putting themselves last
- Making it hard to differentiate between helping and enabling
- Seeing every conflict or disagreement as negative
- Going along in order to get along
- Doing more than is reasonable to be liked and included
- Feeling not good enough/wondering if they've done enough
- Taking things too personally
- Not being able to say no, and avoiding conflict and confrontation at all costs
- Worrying excessively about what others think
- Taking factual criticism as a personal attack
- Forgiving but not forgetting and the inability to get past rejections, or feeling offended

- Carrying the pain of the world
- _____
- _____

What can make trouble for **Golds**?

- Worrying about change and fearing the unknown
- Showing impatience quite often, in verbal and non-verbal ways
- Being unable to bleed off stress or bounce back from adversity
- Being inflexible, overly focused, and controlled by the to-do list
- Having unreasonably high expectations, causing themselves and others frustration
- Not asking for help or accepting help and seeing this as a sign of weakness
- Having a 'never' and 'always' way of doing things, an attitude of black & white, and a right or wrong mindset
- Never really taking the time to have fun and relax
- Adopting a drill sergeant or bossy-type approach
- Wanting to be Mr. or Mrs. Perfect to the world
- Seeking to be right instead of happy
- Running all those negative 'what if's' and 'what could go wrong' scenarios through their minds
- Planning too much and way too far ahead
- _____
- _____

What can make trouble for **Oranges**?

- Showing their frustrations in inappropriate and noticeable ways
- Saying exactly what's on their minds/having a lack of tact
- Getting too far ahead, too quickly – full speed ahead – no matter what
- Using humor as a defense mechanism at inappropriate times

- Displaying impatience by finishing someone else's thoughts or sentences
- Cutting others off others due to impatience in listening skills
- Having selective memory and frequent short-term thinking or focus
- Over-committing – having way too many irons in the fire where something may get dropped
- Overlooking details – then re-doing stuff
- Expecting others to be as fast as they are
- Multi-tasking too much and not staying focused or on-task
- Not finishing, following-through, or following-up
- _____
- _____

What can make trouble for **Greens**?
- Being stubborn – needing or wanting to be right
- Jumping to problem-solving or having a fix-it attitude
- Exhibiting sarcasm or a condescending tone of voice
- Putting process ahead of people
- Not letting others 'in', or seeing the real person
- Having little tolerance for small talk
- Making a game of trying to catch people off guard or questioning what they know
- Being too direct with too few words
- Not connecting with others on an emotional or personal level
- Losing trust or credibility in people, groups, or processes
- Over analyzing – analysis paralysis and second guessing themselves constantly
- Being impatient with people who 'just don't get it'
- Displaying their Green (non-emotional) poker face
- _____
- _____

Communicating By E-mail

From: George Boelcke [mailto:george@vantageseminars.com]
Sent: Every day   To: Every Color

Working in the oil-patch, a retail shop, or simply out in the field, we may be lucky enough not to have to deal with a barrage of e-mails every hour of every day. Unfortunately, for the rest of the world, e-mail is the primary means of communication in almost every company.

While e-mails may be efficient and a great time-management tool for senders, they can also drive recipients crazy. If communication is a big challenge, e-mails will compound that problem every day for every Color.

When we know someone's Color, communicating by e-mail should be in the same fashion that each Color values talking to us in person. In fact, each Color's list of strengths and stresses will give us all the clues we need to effectively communicate with them in writing.

The people-first Colors of Blue and Orange really don't want our e-mails to be a book, sound like their written by a lawyer, or include every single detail. These two Colors value a short personal note and expect us to stay positive – yes, even in e-mails. Moreover, both would rather just get a phone call. It's quicker, requires way less back-and-forth, and let's them talk to a real person, instead of staring at a computer screen. Unfortunately, no matter how often they reply with 'give me a call', they usually just get another e-mail in response.

Golds and Greens are task-first Colors who look for specific facts, details, and all the relevant information – in their conversations and meetings, and in writing. Neither Color is interested in too much personal stuff beyond one or two lines. When an e-mail starts a long chain of back and forth questions, Golds would rather get a call.

One call will often avoid adding six more e-mails on their to-do lists. E-mails, specifically, affect the Colors in various different ways:

Blues live life through their feelings and making intuitive decisions. Their preference is to talk to someone face to face where they can actually make eye contact and where their intuition works best.

Unfortunately, things can go off track in e-mails when Blues attempt to interpret tones or feelings, rather than just focusing on the factual content. To other Colors, receiving an all-capitalized note is just seen as rude and poor-mannered. However, for Blues it's very hurtful; it really does seem like someone is standing in front of them and yelling.

As a result, they often wonder why someone sent such a 'cold' or 'rude' e-mail, or if they are mad at them. It isn't logical. But then, while feelings aren't about logic, they're just as valid. If other Colors don't accept that about Blues, they are in for a lifetime of misunderstandings and conflict.

Blues look to connect with others, even by e-mail. They share one or two lines about themselves and may wish the receiver a great weekend. This small talk goes a very long way with this Color. Other Colors should boost up their language when writing to a Blue: using "awesome" instead of "good", or "great" instead of "fine". By caring about Blues, and by speaking their *language* – in as much the same way as they naturally care about others – will pay off in measurable ways.

For Blues, other Colors must make an effort to focus the first part of e-mails on the people impacts – the issues which will help customers, vendors, or their teams. As for the remainder of the e-mail, Blues function in the same *Gold* environment as every other Color does, and will look for details, actionable tasks, and specific instructions.

Golds look for closure and getting things off their to-do lists. This certainly includes e-mails, as there's nothing better than an (almost) empty in box. They look for specifics and clearly defined subjects. If they're covering more than one issue, they prefer to have separate correspondences, as this will allow Golds to deal with one matter in one e-mail at a time. It will also allow them to file e-mails in their proper places.

Yes, they do retain a ton of e-mails, partly to have proper paper trails, and partly to keep as evidence down the road... Whatever we do, we must make sure that we have a specific subject line for those same reasons, particularly to help Golds efficiently track any subsequent correspondences.

Golds also have a propensity for sending follow-up messages. Did you get this? Do you have an answer yet? Just confirming... are e-mails that can drive other Colors crazy. Why do they do it? Because an issue or task is on the to-do list, and until we deal with it and get back to them – it can't come off their list! Until then, Golds are in a hurry-up-and-wait mode.

One other heads-up for fellow Golds: think about the other Colors, not just the Gold's own preferences, before pressing the reply button just to confirm an e-mail was received. The world defaults to the assumption that the email *was* received. While Golds want to acknowledge it and be polite and responsible, the other Colors would prefer no response.

Oranges want others to get to the point quickly – be brief, be bright, be done. E-mails should never be longer than the screen view. Yet, Oranges continue to read to pages three, four, and five, all the while feeling they are getting carpel tunnel syndrome from all the scrolling. Oranges realize in the back of their minds that they may miss something important so they continue to scan the world's longest message to try and catch the highlights.

Since Oranges are quite good at multi-tasking, it helps to remember that they are likely to be reading our notes on the move, during meetings, or in between other tasks. In an ideal world, Oranges would love e-mails to be capped at roughly the same maximum 140 characters as a Twitter tweet.

Oranges also have a gift of being able to separate the important from the mundane and to focus on immediate issues, rather than anything that can be put off until next week. As a result, they can be quite selective with which e-mails they'll open right away. If we'd like their attention and a quick response, we must make sure the subject line has something which will give them reason to read ours, before the 50 (and rising) others from which they can choose.

Oranges are very aware that e-mails are a constant drain on their time. We should make sure to not send unnecessary messages, or messages with a lot of links and attachments. If they find that our e-mails consistently aren't important or relevant, we will inadvertently teach them to ignore our messages.

Greens look for credibility. Through e-mails, this means that correct grammar and spelling are not optional. If our texts have words underlined in red – fix them before pressing the send button! Greens find it difficult to read e-mails with mistakes in grammar, and that does not reflect well on our credibility. It will affect the way they view the rest of the content, hinder their interpretation of what we're asking for, and perhaps negatively shape their reply. In fact, some Greens, when viewing e-mails they need to retain, will forward it back to themselves after first fixing the spelling errors.

E-mails are actually the preferred communication method for Greens, especially on important matters or issues involving complex decisions. They allow Greens to be in control of when to press reply, which only happens when they've had the chance to think through the issues or implications, and have completed their homework first.

Just as their e-mails are succinct, short, factual, and direct – we must keep ours the same way. There is no need for us to build relationships or get personal – just get to the point. And please, please, we must remember not to add in any *lol's*. It drives Greens crazy. If it's funny, they'll be able to discern it. If not, the need to point it out won't make it so.

It also may help to know that Greens will frequently skip any e-mails which are cc'd to them. Their attitudes are: if it's not *to* me or *for* me, don't bother me. Greens deem that most cc'd e-mails are simply someone's attempt to cover their butt or to boast to as many people as possible.

Conflict: Stuff Happens

*One of our greatest strengths is the
acknowledgement of our shortcomings.*

Can we think of something we can do, starting tomorrow, that'll make
things worse in our relationships with our coworkers? Of course –
we all can. Can we think of some things that'll make our lives better?
Certainly! Colors is a significant tool to be able to accomplish that.

The majority of workplace conflicts arise out of a Colors clash.
Following this, the issues can often escalate because of the
behavioral choices of our Colors.

From passive-aggressive moods, subtle comments or behaviors,
to full-out verbal assaults, conflict comes in many ways – and Colors.
How we choose to deal with conflict is commonly reflective of our
Colors. In stress or conflict situations, people tend to go into their
secondary Colors in order to deal with these problems. Consequently,
any conflict-resolution coaching template which is not based on
personality types has no chance of success.

Should conflict be avoided at all cost? Is it a reason to shut someone
down? Is it perhaps a healthy way to express different opinions,
argue a case, or grow trusting and stronger teams, all pulling in
the same direction as a result?

Let's look at an example. Logic-first Colors (higher Green than Blue)
want to debate an issue. They look at rationally discussing things,
mulling the options on the table, and coming up with better
solutions or new information and processes. It's not about feelings,
and disagreements do not have much of an impact on this group.
They view conflict resolution as more of a debriefing. What *does*
concern high Greens is if the conversation turns into an emotional
discussion and becomes irrational, as they perceive it.

Conversely, the feelings-first Colors (higher Blue than Green) see
conflict in a very different way. Conflict triggers an emotional

reaction, increases stress, and builds anxiety. This group will often be afraid to say something in fear of escalating the situation and damaging or jeopardizing their relationships.

Oranges prefer to have any conflict dealt with quickly so they can move on. They can say a lot, and maybe not always in full sentences, and they often don't take the feelings of others into account. They can make many points on all kinds of issues, but may not remember them all later. Oranges are often surprised when others repeat things back to them that they have said.

Oranges often can't remember all of the points, may deny they even said some of them, and certainly don't see how others get hooked on every little detailed comment. They are just throwing out ideas and comments to see what would stick, what's on point, or what may be useful in resolving the matter.

Golds and Greens can become frustrated with these types of conversations. They may withdraw or shut down, get defensive, or just shake their heads. They look for complete thoughts which can be discussed, used, or rejected *before* moving on. Please – one point at a time and no machine-gun type approach. This group may want to *help* Oranges to focus, or to remind them that they *did* say that. However, that drive often makes things worse, and totally sidetracks the issue. At that point, resolving the issue gets pushed entirely off the rails when both sides begin focusing more on proving that they are right.

Blues and Oranges can tell by our faces if something is wrong. Since they are more instinctive, they are often better at reading people. With Golds and Greens we have to tell them.

Regardless of our Colors, when we're done feeling ticked off, hurt, or angry, we must take accountability for our actions and consider what we could have done differently, could have done better, or could have done more of. It's an important step, because there will always be a next time. When we're choosing an action, we're also choosing a result. And when we're choosing a behavior, we're also choosing a consequence.

Our first reaction to a disagreement or conflict may do more damage than good when we start to play one of our self-defeating games of: get them before they get us, get angry, shut down, do the silent treatment, gossip or lie, evade or deny, quit on ourselves, quit on our teams, stop cooperating, stop giving 100% effort, or leave our jobs entirely. All of these are really self-defeating practices that don't accomplish anything to help solve an issue.

Three useless conversation points in a conflict:
Irrelevant: Better late than not showing up at all...
Comparison: That's not as serious as you doing...
Historical: Well last month you...

A good rule of thumb to remember is that anything we say before taking responsibility is perceived as an excuse. If it occurs afterwards, it is usually seen as an explanation.

Blame avoids accountability. It's not as though we, or someone on our teams, are the first people to ever do something wrong. It started in the Garden of Eden when Adam wouldn't admit he ate the fruit...

Sadly, personal accountability is becoming quite rare. But if we do choose the mindset of being accountable for our actions, we'd be amazed how the money and promotion police in our companies will find us and may offer us a pay raise or a promotion.

We can do this when we're calm and away from battle. If we could think of two things we might do differently, we could prevent a situation from escalating to a fight, strong words, or an argument. We could own up to it, suck it up, and patch it up. We would choose to be happy more often than wanting to be right. It really is possible to disagree without being disagreeable, and our attitudes always control our altitudes.

Before or during our efforts to resolve a disagreement or conflict, are we first remembering the other person's Colors and being aware of their *language*, feelings, and approach to conflict resolution?

Did we get what someone else was saying, or just hear the words?

Are we building our rebuttal half way through someone's point?

Do we get defensive first, or play offense in driving to get this resolved and agreed to?

How much time, or how many times, do we need to backtrack, and wish we could take back our words or actions?

Are we cognisant of what we're feeling inside? Perhaps it's feeling scared, hurt, defensive, judged, or attacked? How are these feelings coming across in our words, tone of voice, or body language?

Do we sometimes give in just to end up resentful later?

Can we avoid the comment of *whatever*?

Is our primary focus on being right or being happy?

Are we driven to accomplish a win, or to reach a win-win?

Do we hide behind an either-or approach or quote policy rather than manage a special situation?

Do we sometimes just want to accomplish making another person feel stupid, uninformed, or wrong?

Will we finish one complete thought or idea and allow others some input before moving on?

Do we feel the need to sometimes escalate the conflict, or move back to black or white thinking?

What are the trigger points when we shut down, give up, or give in?

At what point can we focus on the benefit of the end result versus the current battle?

Could we repeat back what someone else said? It may be very different than what we actually heard.

Are we saying the right things in a kind way?

Are we being smart without being a smart-ass?

Do we raise our voices? It does not raise the quality of our feedback or comments.

In the heat of the moment, will we recognize the time when it's best to say nothing at all?

Do we attempt to simply put out the fire or also to focus on preventing future fires?

Is our input helpful or hurtful?

Disagreements and conflicts happen every day and on every team and in every relationship. Whether they contribute to our growth and the growth of our teams, or cause hurt feelings and job dissatisfaction, it's up to us.

We'll learn more from people we disagree with than those we agree with.

We need to remember that there are more than seven billion people in the world, and there isn't another person in the whole world that will agree with us, or think exactly the same way as us, on everything. This makes it critical to remember and to understand that disagreement does not equal rejection.

Often, caring about others means *not* telling them what they want to hear. It's being honest enough to tell them the truth and by being as direct as possible. After all, others (and us too) cannot change, or heal what they don't know or acknowledge.

The Mind-body connection

For most people, and for every Color, conflict creates stress either at the time of the conflict or for a long time after.

A recent story in *Family Health*, written by Dr. Robin Reesal, a professor of psychiatry, drew some great connections between what our minds experience and how these experiences manifest themselves in our bodies. And yes, there is a proven connection.

What are some of the internal stressors that may be sending distress signal to our bodies? First and foremost, it is always critical to rule out any physical symptoms unrelated to these possible mind-body experiences. Then, we need to analyze – and doctors often (should) ask – what's really going on in our lives.

Of course, we often use denial to keep our emotions in check. And the more we ignore these signals, our early warning systems in our bodies, the more likely our bodies are left with no option but to physically tell us that there's trouble.

Golds and Blues can be amongst the first Colors who find themselves in exactly this position of starting to show physical symptoms of stress, hurt, anger, or burnout, from suppressed feelings of frustration. But it's important to learn and practice a powerful saying coined by *Choices Seminars* founder Thelma Box, "Feelings buried alive never die!"

Similarly, in the words of Dr. Reesal, "We turn our emotional suffering into physical symptoms to avoid facing our troubles". And that's often after many of us try sleeping pills, alcohol, or other vices to attempt to relieve these stresses.

What the mind suppresses – the body expresses

Choose to Grow – Help Is Here

Help! is usually one of the last things we or anyone else on our teams tend to say out loud. But why? Or better yet, why not?

Self-improvement and a desire to grow and learn are the key building blocks to success, which can lead to an increase in pay or responsibilities, or a chance for promotion. This growth can *begin* when we simply admit we don't know something, or ask for help, when we really do need it.

Unfortunately, most Colors seldom ask. Blues are contrary to this norm. Blues are the ones who are most likely to ask for help. However, when they do, it can often be perceived as a sign of weakness or incompetence, which is not only patently false, but also damaging to every other person who also take their clues from the subsequent actions or reactions of others. Whether it is perception or reality, everyone on our teams must either build the courage to keep asking for help, or willingly offer help to others by providing feedback, training, suggestions, support, or input.

Our careers do not have a remote.
We actually have to get up and change things ourselves!

In the first few months on any new job we have to ask numerous questions and get help in several different ways whether we want to or not. Since we're the new person, it goes without saying that we need to ask things of anyone, at any time, regardless of how major or minor the question.

Successful companies are likely to have specific orientations or on-boarding programs. Studies prove that within those companies, employees are 58% more likely to still be with the company three years later. On the other hand, up to 30% of new hires quit within the first year when they do not feel included, connected, or involved. That becomes extremely counterproductive and very expensive for corporations.

According to an Aberdeen Group study, the cost to lose and replace employees is an average of three times their yearly salaries. Clearly then, companies must invest a lot of time, energy, and resources into training. Many companies should even have a significant amount of money which every employee can draw from over a calendar year. Yet in companies that do offer this, many of them don't even spend half of the allocated funds.

Competence = confidence = compensation

At some point in time, the impetus is on us to continue the drive to learn, grow, and ask for help. However, after about three months there seems to be an unwritten rule for most of us, that asking for help is no longer acceptable. Just three short months later we all seem to have forgotten how helpful everyone was! They still are helpful – but we just stopped asking. If we just asked, all those same people would continue to help us grow and learn. They would love to be our cheerleaders, go-to people or mentors – if we just asked.

All four Colors love to help others. The only differences are the specific ways each Color does it. Blues are hard-wired to care about people. They will always put others ahead of their to-do lists. Being helpful to others is a huge way to grow their self-esteem, one of their biggest payoffs.

Golds function out of a sense of duty and responsibility. As the largest groups of volunteers, it stands to reason they are more than happy to help others become more efficient, gain knowledge, or take on more responsibility. They may not be the most approachable while they're in the middle of a task, but they will be more than happy to get together with others to set up a plan and map out a strategy.

The DNA within Greens contains a lifelong drive to learn and grow. As they love to learn, the natural extension of that is to then teach others. Getting others to see the limitless opportunities for growth is at the core of Greens making the world a little better, and a lot smarter.

Oranges, just like their Blue coworkers, are the other people-first Color. Coaching others is a great way to perhaps take some of the workload from them, and to make their entire teams faster, better, and smarter. Besides, coaching others or stepping in to help is often a welcome distraction from some of the work they're currently stuck doing. Oranges are very flexible in their priorities, so there certainly won't be a problem catching them here and there for a few minutes.

Coaching is not just part of the job description of our bosses or our Training and Development departments. It is everyone's responsibility to choose to want to grow, to learn, and to move forward and not backwards. And most of all, not becoming stagnant, is vital.

We would be amazed if we only knew how many people – in all the four Colors – would love to help, coach, and mentor us. But we actually have to do two things: We have to want and ask for help, and we actually have to listen to the feedback. For most of us, that can be easier said than done.

When we take ourselves out of the decision equation, we'll always make the right decision by asking for help or feedback. In other words, let's look at it from an outsider's perspective without first considering our egos, image, or reputation. Let's look to what others may think, and not worry about the perception (not reality) of looking weak.

By seeking assistance, we get past our negative attitudes towards changes. This helps us to overcome our obstacles each step of the way:

I won't...
I can't...
I want to...
How do I do it?...
I'll try...
I can...
I will...
Yay! I did it!

... omitting the internal voice of "I'm scared to try..." and then looking back and thinking: That wasn't hard at all – and so worth it!

"Take out your resume and look at it. If it's the same as last year, you're not growing. We don't want you to leave, but we don't need one year's experience 20 times, we need 20 years experience."
John Gibson, CEO – Tervita Corp.

Bumblebees Can't Fly

It's true. Experts say it's aerodynamically impossible. It is just that someone forgot to tell the bumblebee. Is that true for us at work and in our careers? What do we think we can't do? What things do we just accept without question? But if we knew we couldn't fail – what would we do differently?

Are we making real decisions or just following our fixed beliefs? What is just outside our comfort zone, in terms of work success, personal growth, or the skills we need for our next promotion? It's not called a comfort zone because it's comfortable. It's called a comfort zone because it's uncomfortable to step out of it! And when we want something we've never had, we have to do some things we've never done.

At times, others at work are fighting harder for us than we're prepared to fight for ourselves. Really! We just don't see it – and there is a limit to how long they'll do it. From our Training and Development departments, to suggestions by others on our teams, to our supervisors or managers – we need to start looking for it and we'll begin to see people all around us who want us to grow and succeed!

Safety Success Through Colors

Working safely and ensuring that everyone on our teams makes it home safely every night is one of the core values for every company and every Color. Each Color's core strengths contain some specialties they contribute to the safety of their teams:

Blues are naturally talented at being...

Creative: Finding innovative ways in helping others work safely.

Flexible: Being very adaptable to new and improved ways.

Great listeners: Fully understanding the coaching techniques and instructions and 'translating' them into user-friendly steps for their teams.

Intuitive: Sensing when something isn't right and knowing quickly when others don't understand.

People-first: Working together, succeeding together, and keeping each other safe at all times. They are always there when someone needs a hand, an hour, or an assist.

... Blues can use help in not avoiding conflict. Safety is about helping their buddies and not the time to go along in order to get along. It's OK to speak up as they'll be helping, not hurting others.

Golds are naturally talented at being...

Black or white focused: Following policies and rules to the letter – every job, every person, every day. No exception, no shortcuts. One safety incident is one too many.

Detail oriented: Getting it done means it'll be done right, and by the book. Safety is in the little things, 20 times a day if required.

Giving & helpful: Taking the time to coach others and never defaulting to an 'it's not my job' attitude. We succeed safely and together.

Practical: Translating safety rules effectively into concrete and specific, practical steps for teams to implement and follow.

Self-motivated: Taking ownership of policies and issues. Golds do what's right even when nobody is looking, and will hold others on their team accountable for their actions (or lack thereof).

... Golds can use help in not over-worrying, and with their common reluctance to change routines or processes. Improvements make things safer and are worth it, and others will be there to help with the implementation.

Oranges are naturally talented at being...

Direct: Willing to say what needs to be said and holding their buddies accountable for safety first. Others will not be missing the feedback or meaning.

Flexible: Being very fast on their feet and quick to adapt to better procedures. Oranges are open-minded and never stuck in the past.

Positive & Just Doing It: Finding ways to implement complex safety procedures and making them work, no matter what. Stop complaining, let's get on with it and make it happen.

Skillful & hands-on: Finding innovative solutions that matter, and being very creative without impacting productivity or wasting time.

Winners: Any day and every day that is incident-free is a win, and they are a big part of it. Hazard hunts (pro-actively finding any hazard on a job site) is a BIG game they'll undertake and probably win.

... Oranges can use help in having others watch their speed and impatience. Fast can turn to trouble and safety is more about the small issues and steps than the big picture. It's helpful for others to remind them that slowing down really will speed them up.

Greens are naturally talented at being...

Factual & logical: Always thinking before acting (or working), staying focused on logical steps, reasoning and factual of what's happening, and not making excuses or taking shortcuts.

Knowledgeable: Learning and paying it forward by teaching others. Greens value being the go-to people for continuous coaching, and offering feedback for improvements and solutions.

Problem-solvers: Taking complex policies, obstacles or challenges and finding the best ways to implement them or correct them.

Question-askers: Probing, questioning, and asking the 'what about' and 'what if' questions. Their drive for perfection will keep them asking and innovating.

Skilled: Independently finding innovative and improved processes and solutions others may not see or think about.

... Greens can use help in holding themselves accountable to work within existing safety rules, even those they believe should be better or don't make sense. After all, their leadership skills can set the example for their teammates.

"We can only operate at the speed at which we can be safe."
John Gibson, CEO – Tervita Corp.

Finding Work-Life Balance

For all Colors of people, especially for Blues and Golds, finding the balance between work life and personal life is often a real challenge. And while it also may be a part of the values and the mission statements within many companies, it is a principle that may be easier said than done.

An old commencements address at Georgia Tech from Brian Dyson, the former President and CEO of Coca-Cola may help put some perspective on work-life balance:

Imagine life as a game in which you are juggling some five balls in the air. You name them – work, family, health, friends and spirit... and you're keeping all of these in the air.

You will soon understand that work is a rubber ball. If you drop it, it will bounce back. But the other four balls – family, health, friends and spirit – are made of glass. If you drop one of these, they will be irrevocably scuffed, marked, nicked, damaged, or even shattered. They will never be the same. You must understand that and strive for balance in your life. How?

Don't undermine your worth by comparing yourself to others. It is because we are different that each of us is special.

Don't set your goals by what other people deem important. Only you know what is best for you.

Don't take for granted the things closest to your heart. Cling to them as you would your life, for without them, your life is meaningless.

Don't let your life slip through your fingers by living in the past or for the future. By living your life one day at a time, you live all the days of your life.

Don't give up when you still have something to give. Nothing is really over until the moment you stop trying.

Don't be afraid to admit that you are less than perfect. It is this fragile thread that binds us to each together.

Don't be afraid to encounter risks. It is by taking chances that we learn how to be brave.

Don't shut love out of your life by saying it's impossible to find time. The quickest way to receive love is to give it; the fastest way to lose love is to hold it too tightly; and the best way to keep love is to give it wings!

Don't run through life so fast that you forget not only where you've been, but also where you are going.

Don't forget, a person's greatest emotional need is to feel appreciated.

Don't be afraid to learn. Knowledge is weightless, a treasure you can always carry easily.

Don't use time or words carelessly. Neither can be retrieved. Life is not a race, but a journey to be savoured each step of the way.

— used with permission